Leadership is an Inside Job

Why Character is the Key to Effective Leadership

by

Jim T. Priest, J.D.

DORRANCE
PUBLISHING CO
EST. 1920
PITTSBURGH, PENNSYLVANIA 15238

Dorrance Publishing Co
585 Alpha Drive
Suite 103
Pittsburgh, PA 15238
Visit our website at *www.dorrancebookstore.com*

ISBN: 979-8-8860-4098-2
eISBN: 979-8-8860-4997-8

DEDICATION

So many people have influenced my views and practices on leadership my desire is to dedicate this book to <u>*all*</u> of them. But a singular and enormous debt of gratitude is owed to my Dad, Ted Priest, for living a life worth imitating. So this is especially dedicated in his memory and for the glory of God. ***Deo gratias.***

WHAT PEOPLE ARE SAYING ABOUT
Leadership is an Inside Job

If I could I would connect a balloon to Jim Priest's book on leadership so it would float high enough for everyone to see and read it. Jim Priest and his friend Reggie Whitten have been friends of mine and fellow world changers for years. Their efforts to help others cover many human needs and stretch well beyond Oklahoma. Jim's book is another effort to positively change the world.

- Bob Goff, Chief Balloon Inflator and *New York Times* bestselling author *Love Does; Everybody, Always; Dream Big; and Undistracted.*

With anecdotes and hard-earned insights from decades of leadership, Jim Priest reminds us that at its core, leadership is service. Jim paints a picture for the reader of what true leadership looks like and offers guidance for those looking to harness its power by tapping into both ageless wisdom and personal experience. *Leadership is an Inside Job* is a must read for anyone looking to ground themselves in rock solid principles and eager to lead by example.

- Steve Preston, President and CEO, Goodwill Industries International.

It's been a honor and privilege to be part of Jim's ecosystem these last 30 years. Jim always brings humility, humor and humanity to his leadership and advice. This book is no exception. I've had the privilege of working with some great leaders and been part of an organization that practices servant leadership. Jim's practical perspective and ability to simplify the core principles of a leader is outstanding and hits the bulleye! I'm thrilled his insights will now be available for everyone.

- Anne Bramman, Chief Financial Officer, Nordstrom

Jim Priest is a personal friend who is a leader of leaders. His contributions through writing, teaching, and advocacy have greatly benefitted the health of families and the development of leaders. His wisdom is pertinent and timely for such a time as this.

- David A. Busic, M.Div., D.D., D.Min. General Superintendent Church of the Nazarene

Leadership is an Inside Job is refreshing new look at a subject few know better than Jim Priest. His decades of work on this topic remind us that leadership must constantly be studied and refined. Anyone looking for opportunities to make a difference will benefit from Jim's wisdom and writing abilities. Here's hoping this book finds principled readers looking for positive energy and motivation.

- Mick Cornett, Former Mayor of Oklahoma City 2004-2018

Knowing Jim Priest as a leader in the business sector, as a community volunteer, and as the CEO of a significant nonprofit organization, I can say without hesitation that he exemplifies the principles discussed in *Leadership is an Inside Job*. Jim gives real-life examples of these essential leadership attributes which supplies valuable insight for those who lead organizations, businesses, and communities. This is a book to share with those who are, or aspire to be, change agents.

- Ann Ackerman, Ph.D. CEO of Leadership Oklahoma (2006-2015)

Jim Priest is the ideal person to write about leadership. I have watched his life for 30 years, first as a successful trial lawyer, and for the past decade, CEO of Oklahoma non-profits. He has demonstrated the leadership qualities which he advances in this book. The principles in this book will make you a more effective leader, no matter if you are the leader of your family or the leader of a large organization.

- Bob Burke, Constitutional Lawyer and Author

In the pages of this book, you will find a reliable map for charting a course for success. With intentional brevity, Jim presents his concepts clearly and succinctly. Each word has been carefully chosen. The result of Jim's effort is a highly readable and practical book. Jim is a bridge. He connects people and ideas. As a result, Jim has been able to consistently build (or strengthen) healthy and effective teams. This book is yet another example of how Jim uses his life experiences and re-markable ability to communicate to help others thrive.

- Dr. Nathan Mellor CEO of Strata Leadership

After knowing Jim Priest for more than four decades I can swear to tell the truth, the whole truth and nothing but the truth: Jim practices what he preaches and lives the outstanding advice he gives in this book. I'll also warn you, he thinks he's funny, but I'll let you decide about that.

- Reggie Whitten, co-founder of the Whitten Burrage law firm and nationally recognized trial lawyer

SAGE COUNSEL

IMPARTING WISDOM ▲ IMPACTING LIVES

INTRODUCTION

There are so many books about leadership, it seems foolish to add one more. But I love to write and I love the subject of leadership. Most of all, I love teaching and mentoring leaders. While I am reluctant to burden reading lists with yet one more book on leadership, I am compelled by my mission to offer this book as a potentially helpful tool in your quest to become a better leader. My conviction is leadership is an inside job. It's about character qualities you can cultivate.

I practiced employment and civil rights law as a trial attorney for thirty-five years. During that time, I discovered, through my clients' experiences, what works and what doesn't. I've had a front row seat (often in the courtroom) to observe the challenges of leading organizations and employees. I have also served three nonprofit organizations and served on the boards of many others. I've been a pastor, a church leader, a community leader, and a candidate for statewide public office.

As you'll see in Part Three, I started in a leadership position at a young age—and failed miserably. I thought being a leader meant bossing people around. Was I wrong! There are so many facets of leadership, although the majority of it focuses on relationships. If you don't like, care for, and want to serve people, you're doomed as a leader. You might have a title, but you won't be a leader in the best sense of that word. At its core, leadership is about serving others.

I offer this book in three parts. Part 1 deals with 21 Leadership Principles that I have tried to practice and commend to others for consideration and adoption. Part 2 is an edited transcript of a presentation entitled The H*I*G*H*way of Success in which I discuss how the Old Testament patriarch, Joseph, experienced success through four character qualities while enduring disheartening and life threatening adversity. Part 3 is a podcast interview I did with Dr. Nathan Mellor of Strata Leadership in which I discuss my history and ideas about leadership.

PART 1

Priest's 21 Principles of Leadership

Originally I put together these leadership principles in order to help employees with whom I work better understand my overall operating philosophy. As a CEO, I sometimes make decisions that make employees scratch their heads and say, "Why did he do THAT?" My hope was, by reading these principles, everyone would grasp the framework of my decision making and leadership style and better understand my decisions. I wanted people to know there was a method to my madness, so they could understand the basis of the things I say and do and decisions I make. These are some of the principles I live and lead by, and while I do not mandate employees follow them, I encourage people to adopt them as their own.

These are **leadership** principles, and some who read these may think to themselves, I'm not a leader. But think again. Whether you realize it or not, you **are** a leader. It may not feel that way sometimes but you are. We all have a circle of influence. Someone (or some group) is looking to us as an example, and to those people, we are a leader.

When I was a little kid, my mom would always send me out the door to school in the morning with this reminder, "Remember, Jimmy, someone is always watching you!" At the time, I thought it meant she had other moms out there spying on me! (She probably did!) But what she really meant was that someone was looking to me as an example. The same is true for you. Whether we realize it or not, we are an example. Is it a positive one? Let's give them an exemplary person to watch and a role model to follow. Remember what Mom Priest said, someone is always watching you!

I have organized these principles into three groups of seven: personal, functional, and relational. Clearly there is overlap, and many could be reclassified into one of the other categories. But you'll get the idea.

THE 21 PRINCIPLES CATEGORIZED

Personal

- Core Values
- Integrity
- Humor
- Teachable
- Creative
- Margin
- Humility

Functional

- Focus
- Delegate
- Team
- Confidentiality
- Bottom Line
- Informal / Perfect
- Bias for Action

Relational

- Employees First
- Listen Well
- Treat like Adults
- Other Oriented
- Mess Up / Fess Up
- Conflict
- Prioritize

PERSONAL LEADERSHIP PRINICPLE 1:

Core Values

At the heart of all good leadership are core values. What is the internal compass that gives you direction? What are the main things you want to be remembered for at the end of your life? If you do not have core values that are "top of mind" and guide your life, you are liable to drift without purpose or conviction or be unduly influenced by others.

My three core values—and the three things I'd like chiseled on my tombstone when I die—are these: Integrity, Encouragement, Enthusiasm.

Integrity is being the same kind of person whether or not someone is looking. It means being a "whole"—integrated—person. Not two faced. Not swayed by the opinions of others. Steady, reliable, trustworthy, and always consistent.

Encouragement means to put courage into others. To help them be their best. To praise them in pubic and critique them, if necessary, in private.

Enthusiasm means more than cheerleader, rah-rah hype. The root word of enthusiasm is the Greek word *En Theos*, meaning "in God." I want to be a cheerleader for people, but I want to be more than that. I want people to see God reflected in the way I live and lead.

Write down your core values. Make sure you believe them and strive to live them. Write them like you're writing your own obituary.

If you have integrity, nothing else matters. If you don't have integrity, nothing else matters

-Alan Simpson

I strive, imperfectly, to be a person of integrity. Remember when you were back in school in math class and talked about "integers?" The teacher told you that integers were "whole numbers." That's because the root meaning of the word integrity is "wholeness." Which means you are "undivided." So if you are a person of integrity, you are a "whole and undivided person." You are the same kind of person and make the same kind of moral choices, even when nobody is watching.

Most of us know the right thing(s) to do, but sometimes our ethical choices are not so clear. Each day we face a variety of ethical decisions, some affecting us, some affecting our family, some affecting others. If you are ever unclear about the ethics or morality of something, just ask. Talk with a supervisor or call the HR department.

Usually our integrity is initially compromised in the small things. We don't wake up in the morning and say to ourselves, "I think I'll rob a bank today." More often we are faced with small compromises of our integrity: to gossip, to cheat on something small, to tell a half truth.

C.S. Lewis, a famous author and theologian, once wrote, *"The safest road to hell is the gradual one - the gentle slope, soft underfoot, without sudden turnings, without milestones, without signposts."* What he was saying was we must resist the temptation to compromise in small things because small compromises will ultimately lead to bigger ones. Never allow your decisions, great or small, to dilute your personal integrity or the integrity of your organization.

PERSONAL LEADERSHIP PRINICPLE 3:

Humor

I believe humor is the oil in the engine of life. By this I mean tasteful, respectful humor. Take your work seriously, but don't take yourself too seriously.

I like to use humor in the workplace, in speeches, and in my personal life. It lightens the mood. It creates the lubricant of laughter. I especially like poking fun at myself (and there is plenty to poke fun at). There are some times and some issues that are sobering and must be approached seriously, but many times we can bridge the communication gap with others by using appropriate humor.

Remember the emphasis is on appropriate humor. We should NEVER misuse humor by being crude, offensive, or to demean someone. I was a lawyer for over thirty years and spent much of my time handling cases of workplace harassment that ended up in lawsuits. Most of those cases started out by someone joking in an inappropriate way. If you have any question about whether you should tell that joke, or you get a sense that people are offended by your use of humor, just knock it off and apologize.

PERSONAL LEADERSHIP PRINICPLE 4:

Teachable

I personally want to be—and I would like all of our team members to be—approachable and teachable. If I am doing something wrong or have unintentionally offended someone, I want to hear about it. I also want to learn from others and am always open to being taught. Author Brandon Triola writes:

> *I've had lunch with millionaires. I've eaten with celebrities, successful musicians, authors, and more. In all my run-ins with people who ride the wave of life through ups and downs and still manage to come out on top of the water–their keys to success*

*are always similar, simple, and powerful. I have
noticed something astonishing about all of them
—**They're all teachable.***

Approachable and teachable means being open. I want to be someone who others are not afraid to approach with a corrective suggestion or critique. It means being humble. Not thinking more of yourself (or less of yourself) than you should (see *Humility*). It means being willing to listen and learn, even from someone you think knows less than you (many times you find out they actually know more than you.)

PERSONAL LEADERSHIP PRINICPLE 5:

Creative

I try to cultivate creativity and want to suggest to you that YOU can be creative. You may not think of yourself as "creative," but you are! You were creative when you were a kid, so you just need to get your creative juices flowing again. Try new ways of looking at things, and don't be afraid to come up with "crazy" ideas. Take a different route to work. Do something/anything to disrupt your routine!

Walt Disney, the creative genius who dreamed up Mickey Mouse, Donald Duck, and Disney theme parks, was constantly working on ideas that seemed crazy and out of the box. In fact if he brought up a new idea at a board meeting, and it was not *opposed by everyone*, Disney concluded the idea was not creative enough and he abandoned the project.

We should not just think "outside the box"—sometimes we should completely throw away the box. The way to come up with good ideas is to come up with *a lot* of ideas and throw out the bad ones. So don't be reluctant to think of something new and creative. For more information on this, see the book *A Kick in the Seat of the Pants* by Roger Von Oech (and his second book, *A Whack in the Side of the Head*).

PERSONAL LEADERSHIP PRINICPLE 6:
Margin

Have you ever noticed those lines on the left and right side of notebook paper? They are called "margins." Generally you are not supposed to write in those margins, but on occasion it's okay to do so. The margins are there to keep you balanced on the paper and to keep you from constantly going off the edge. We need margins in our lives to keep us from going off the edge, too. We need to strive for balance between our work lives and our non-work lives. I do not believe any organization should consistently overwork its people, and I strive to insure people on my team are all working hard—but not having our hair on fire all the time. We must live with "margin," which means that we do not constantly work to the limits, and beyond the limits, of our time and energy. Occasionally certain seasons of the year or projects will come along that "max us out"—but we do not want people consistently working at or beyond the limits of their capacity. If we have overloaded a team member, we need to hire help or narrow what we do. For more information on this concept, see Richard Swenson's excellent book, *Margin*.

Humility is not thinking less of yourself, **but thinking** of yourself less.

-C.S. Lewis

None of us is perfect (see "relaxed style/perfect performance" below), and we all have many things to learn. I strive to stay humble and respectful of all people, regardless of their place on the social ladder or organizational chart, and I believe humility is a key characteristic to leadership success. Humility does not mean thinking less of yourself, but it means thinking of yourself less often. Humility is inconsistent with cockiness, but it is consistent with confidence. You can be confident in yourself and your ability to do your job and still be humble.

When I was a youngster, there was a lady in our church who frequently sang solos in the morning service. If anyone came up to her after the service and complimented her, she would always say "Oh, no. I wasn't in the best voice today. I wasn't very good." That sounds like humility, but it wasn't. All it did was put more emphasis on herself. This woman seemed incapable of responding to a compliment with confidence and humility. A nice, crisp "Thank you" would have been a sufficient response for the church soloist, even if she *did* think she was not in the best voice.

If you focus on serving others and have a healthy (and not inflated) self-respect for yourself, you can become a humble person. Being humble and showing respect to everyone is an absolute requirement for true success.

FUNCTIONAL LEADERSHIP PRINCIPLE 8:

Focus

You can intend to do good things, but if you try to do too many things, your efforts will fall flat. I believe great leaders begin by identifying the most important things that should be done, writing those down, and staying focused on them until they are accomplished. In my work at Goodwill, I work to be focused and my #1 focus (among the many responsibilities that pull at me) is for us, as an organization, to do all we can to put our employees first. Herb Kelleher, founder of Southwest Airlines, said it well:

"In business school, they'd say, 'This is a real conundrum: Who comes first, your employees, your shareholders, or your customers?' My mother taught me that your employees come first. If you treat them well, then they treat the customers well, and that means your customers come back and your shareholders are happy."

Like Kelleher I have come to believe if organizations treat their employees with respect and care, they will be both relationally successful and financially successful. I have included more about this internal focus under promoting a culture of "Employee First."

FUNCTIONAL LEADERSHIP PRINCIPLE 9:

Delegation

All of us can and should be doing our part—but we must remember we cannot do everything by ourselves and we must partner with others, or delegate responsibility, to reach maximum effectiveness. In organizations I lead, I tell employees, "I will let you do whatever you think you're big enough to do—and I may ask you to do just a little bit more on occasion because personal growth happens when we are challenged to go beyond the limits of what we think we are capable of." Sometimes we must intentionally limit what we do of course. See my comment on "margin." But I believe most of us can do more than we think we can, so if you believe you are not sufficiently challenged in your position, let your supervisor know, and they'll find something to help stretch you!

FUNCTIONAL LEADERSHIP PRINCIPLE 10:

Team

(Together Everyone Achieves More). I am collaborative in my leadership style, and I want collaboration to be infectious throughout our organization and with other organizations in our community. Whatever different responsibilities we have, we should all be pulling on the same oar.

Warren Buffet says an important way to keep employees engaged is to make work purposeful and create an environment of shared values.

Here's an example of what I mean: when my wife and I were raising small children, we had the kids participate in "Saturday morning chores" around the house.

Each of us had chore assignments, but we also had a saying, "We're not done until we're ALL done!" This meant if you finished your chore assignments first, you were to help others with their chores until everyone was finished. This is the kind of attitude and culture that maximizes employee engagement and satisfaction.

FUNCTIONAL LEADERSHIP PRINCIPLE 11:

Confidentiality

Benjamin Franklin said, "Two can keep a secret — if one of them is dead."

When a matter is supposed to be confidential, it should be *strictly* treated that way. I believe in maintaining a confidence unless there is a compelling reason to share information on a need-to-know basis (for example, if someone is threatening to harm themselves or someone else). Otherwise if information is confidential (whether it relates to clients or team members), it should not be shared with anyone, whether that be a fellow team member, a stakeholder, or a spouse.

This is a supremely important rule and must overrule any inclination we have to share confidential information with others.

This means not sharing confidences, even with people you think you can trust or someone who promises to never tell what you told. Do NOT give up confidential information under any circumstances.

FUNCTIONAL LEADERSHIP PRINCIPLE 12:

Give The Bottom Line First

One of the things that comes from spending 35 years as a lawyer is the deep-rooted desire to "cut to the chase" and "get to the point." So whether you are preparing a memo or an email or engaging in a conversation, it's always best to give the "bottom line" first (whether it's a recommendation or conclusion or the ultimate question). If you give the bottom line right up front, you will capture the attention of whomever you're speaking to, and you can then back fill with whatever information is needed to better understand it.

Adopt this same approach with documents prepared for any audience. Cultivate a strong inclination toward short meetings with a written agenda. This is not to say that meetings or conversations need to be "all business" or "brusque," but you can accomplish more in less time if you stay focused and on task.

I've found if you give people the bottom line first—then give them the important information they need—they will listen better to what you have to say. Cut to the chase.

FUNCTIONAL LEADERSHIP PRINCIPLE 13:

Informal in Style, Perfect in Performance

I am a pretty easy person to work with and for; my style is usually rather informal, friendly, and fun. But our relaxed style should never be interpreted as slackness or used as an excuse for less than perfect performance in delivering our work product or services to our community. I like letters and documents to be carefully proof read and "letter perfect" before they go out the door. I want there to be consistency in how we present our services, our logo, and our information to the public. We want to be as near perfect in what we present to the world as possible, recognizing that none of us is perfect and we all make mistakes.

But attention to detail communicates excellence and inspires confidence that we know what we're doing.

As motivational speaker, Larry Winget once said, "Coffee stains on the drop down tray of an airliner makes airline passengers question the engine maintenance." So whether it's the way you speak, your appearance, your correspondence, or the state of your office or building, never give anyone a reason to question your organization's engine maintenance!

FUNCTIONAL LEADERSHIP PRINCIPLE 14:

Bias for Action

I have a bias for action, which means I tend to always lean forward. The signature block on my email closes with "Onward!" That's my motto. And I find more can be accomplished that most of us realize if we have a bias for action.

This has a downside of course. A bias for action can sometimes get too far ahead of planning. A bias for action can sometimes be translated, "Ready, Fire, Aim" with the Fire coming before the Aim. That's where we need everyone checking each other with reality but not drowning dreams with the rain of too much caution. Let's do more than we think we can.

Don't be content with saying, "We don't have the money to do that" or "We've tried that before, it won't work." Take the initiative and and lean forward!

RELATIONAL LEADERSHIP PRINCIPLE 15:

Employees First

The general approach and culture I want to create and to be promoted, is to be servant leaders and put employees/team members first. This does not mean team members are always right or always get their way. What it does mean is placing a high priority on listening well to employees, reinforcing good performance and behavior, and making the organization a place where team members love coming to work (at least most days!).

This principle stands conventional management on its head and is based, in part, on the philosophy of a leader I greatly admire: Herb Kelleher, former president of Southwest Airlines who was mentioned earlier under Focus.

Southwest's first flight was on June 18th, 1971, and the airline initially struggled. That fall the company was losing money with inconsistent ridership. Southwest faced the prospect of either laying off employees or selling a plane.

"We've always taken the approach that employees come first," Kelleher says. **"Happy and pleased employees take care of the customers. And happy customers take care of shareholders by coming back."** So Southwest sold an airplane rather than lay off employees.

Herb's advice to aspiring leaders? **"Be humble; work harder than anyone else; serve your people. I think humility is the most important because if you don't have humility, then the other two—working harder than anyone else and serving your people—probably won't happen. I think you have to be humble and not carried away with your own title or position in order to accomplish the other two."** That's the leader I aspire to be.

RELATIONAL LEADERSHIP PRINCIPLE 16:
Listen Well

I have to admit, this leadership principle is probably the one I need the most work on. Because of my "bias for action," I have a tendency to move first and listen later. I should probably apologize in advance for the times when I do that. I know better, but I don't always do better. But I'm trying. My goal is to be a great listener.

My brother-in-law Scott Davis is a great listener. He leans forward and nods his head when you're talking. He asks questions that make you feel like "he's there." He wants to know more than just the facts. He asks things like, "How did that make you feel?" When I grow up, I want to be more like Scott. Actually I want to be more like Scott right now.

Have you ever been listened to really well? It felt great, didn't it? And you've probably been with people who were not really listening to you. They were looking over your shoulder or sneaking peeks at their cell phone. That feels awful, doesn't it? You can feel they just don't care enough to pay attention.

So let's be good listeners to be good leaders. And if you think I'm not listening to you well enough, you have permission to say, "Jim, are you paying attention?"

RELATIONAL LEADERSHIP PRINCIPLE 17:

Treat People Like Adults

One of the fundamental leadership principles I attempt to follow is to treat people like adults. This means that I expect team members to make responsible decisions and then to live with both the positive and negative consequences of the decisions they make. I believe decisions should be made at the level closest to the situation, and I rarely countermand a decision made by a supervisor.

A related principle is "presume good intent." With the teams I lead, I begin with the assumption that they meant well, even when they make mistakes. Give the benefit of the doubt. Innocent 'til proven guilty. However you phrase it, the idea is to begin with an optimistic mindset of the other person.

If team members make good, well-reasoned decisions, they will enjoy the benefit of those decisions, and if they make unreasonable or immature decisions, they will have to live with the consequences of those decisions. Each individual "owns" the decisions they make and the actions they take.

RELATIONAL LEADERSHIP PRINCIPLE 18:

Other Oriented

Being "other oriented" means we put other people first and are motivated by serving people and not our own self-interest. I want to personally remember our mission, whatever it is, is not about us it's about those we serve. Whether it's the money we spend in programs or on coffee in the office, we want to always keep in mind that we are trustees of the funds and the facilities with which we've been entrusted and we need to be "other oriented" in all we do.

Many years ago, I attended a series of meetings at my church led by a travelling preacher named Stephen Manley. Dr. Manley was a powerful speaker, but unfortunately I recall very little of what he said. Here's what I do remember: during a Saturday morning men's breakfast at a local hotel, we gathered to hear Dr. Manley speak. Manley was seated at the head table, far from where I was, but after everyone was finishing up their bacon and eggs, and before he began to speak, I observed Dr. Manley quietly go around the room with a coffee pot, refilling everyone's coffee mug. Here was the noted preacher—the speaker of the hour—taking on the task of a servant. I have never forgotten that "lesson in the flesh" about being other oriented.

I believe this is an important component of servant leadership; being oriented toward serving others will help us keep our priorities straight.

RELATIONAL LEADERSHIP PRINCIPLE 19:

Mess Up/Fess Up

We all make mistakes, and almost all mistakes can be fixed if they are dealt with promptly. But to fix them, they have to be known. We had a rule at the law firm where I practiced law for many years: if you mess up, fess up immediately.

Don't try to keep mistakes a secret because, as Albert Einstein once said, "The kind of thinking that got you into a problem is not likely the kind of thinking that will get you out of it."

Our natural instinct is to keep our mistakes and errors to ourselves and try to fix them ourselves. I encourage team members not to do that.

Ask for help in problem solving if you mess up, and don't be afraid to admit mistakes. In fact admit them quickly. I have found the quickest route to resolving a problem is to own it, sincerely apologize for it, and then work with others on finding a solution.

RELATIONAL LEADERSHIP PRINCIPLE 20:
Constructive Conflict

As a lawyer dealing with problems in the workplace, I have seen personal conflicts create big problems. But even more often I have seen problems created by people's inability to engage in constructive conflict. Being able to have constructive conflict with co-workers is a crucial key to success for individuals and organizations. Unresolved problems or ignoring issues that won't go away only leaves those problems and issues to fester and get worse.

Conflict has the potential to be constructive but (1) we have to accept and even encourage and embrace a conflict of ideas while (2) not allowing conflict to be personal and destructive. In other words, people have to learn to fight fair. I promote and encourage a constructive conflict of ideas that will lead to better solutions, but everyone must refuse to give in to our natural instinct to avoid or run away from conflict. We must be committed to *constructive and civil* conflict. For more information on the proper approach to conflict, see the book *Crucial Conversations* and *Crucial Confrontations* by Kerry Patterson and Joseph Grenny. The Patterson/Grenny books talk about "accountability," which is part of constructive conflict, and they quote a New York Times best-selling author, Al Switzler:

In the worst organizations, no one holds anyone accountable, In the good organizations, the boss holds people accountable, and in the best organizations, *everyone* **holds** *everyone* **accountable.**

Never be afraid to hold anyone in the organization accountable for their actions.

RELATIONAL LEADERSHIP PRINCIPLE 21:
Prioritize Relationships

Through my years as an attorney, community leader, pastor, and family member, I have come to believe relationship is everything. It's not just "important." For personal and professional success, *everything* hinges on having solid, trusting, caring relationships with those around you and those with whom you interact.

As a lawyer, I was taught to be focused on "transactions." Write the brief. Negotiate the settlement. Win the lawsuit. Meet objectives and accomplish tasks. And above all, keep track of your time so you can bill the client! It isn't so much that relationships were ignored when I was a lawyer, but they weren't prioritized.

Over the years, I have come to believe everything rises and falls on your ability to cultivate and maintain good relationships. With family members, people in your neighborhood, fellow worshippers, clients, vendors, and fellow employees. This is not a simple task. People and relationships have multiple aspects to them, and they are affected by many things over which we have no control: The weather. What a person eats or drinks. Problems they're having in their lives. Trauma from past relationships.

In the limited space available here, the best I can do is emphasize the importance of relationships and encourage you to be intentional about making them a priority. When you start to drift off into a "transactional" state of mind, give yourself a thunk in the head and remember: prioritize relationships.

GOODWILL INDUSTRIES OF CENTRAL OKLAHOMA'S CORE VALUES

INTEGRITY

- Do the right thing
- Be open and truthful
- Uphold our values

INNOVATION

- Seek better ways of doing things
- Welcome ideas
- Learn and Grow

RESPECT

- Listen
- Show care and compassion
- Appreciate the opinions of others

COMMITMENT

- Pursue excellence
- Hold ourselves and others accountable
- Work as a team

As a nonprofit agency, Goodwill is committed to Value Based Leadership and to our four core values listed above. These values align well with the 21 Leadership Principles outlined in this book. The values of the organization you work for should align with your own personal values. If they don't, there will be a tension and unhappiness in your life, and you should consider whether you're in the right organization.

PART 2
THE H*I*G*H*WAY TO SUCCESS:
Honor, Integrity, Grace, Humility

The following is a transcript of a speech I delivered to AT&T employees in Oklahoma City when I was providing legal representation to the company.

Chapter One: The Highway to Success

One of the key principles I consistently try to follow, both in my written and verbal communications, is to speak truth into the marketplace of ideas. That's what I hope to do here. I want to share some truths that have been foundational in my life, and from my observation, in the lives of countless others. I want to highlight four character qualities I am convinced are needed for true success in your personal and professional world.

Just by way of quick background, I grew up in the city of Syracuse in Upstate New York. I had to file for resident alien citizenship and learn to speak the language in Oklahoma after I moved here. Syracuse is a different place from Oklahoma. In Syracuse we have winter about ten months of the year and two months of bad sledding. In Oklahoma, where I moved to begin my law career, the wind blows constantly, tornados are common, and we experience four seasons—sometimes all in the same day.

I grew up in a middle-class blue-collar home. My dad was the president of a local labor union at the General Electric factory. As a result of labor disputes, it seemed we were often on strike. During these strikes, Dad would pick up various odd jobs fixing people's washing machines, kitchen drains, and the like, and I would tag along, learning something of the machine repair trade and carrying the tool box. My father's dad was a miner from the coal fields of Pennsylvania. He started work at the age of eleven and died when he was fifty-five. I never knew my grandpa because he died about two months after I was born. But I know a lot about him. He's been an inspiration to me.

My grandad's dad, my great-grandfather, Teddy Priest, was also a coal miner and died at the age of forty-five. Teddy died in the year 1911 when my granddad was eleven-years-old. I'm told that my great-grandpa died in a mine cave-in at the beginning of the shift. They did not bring him up out of the mine because the company did not want the other miners to stop working. So he lay at the bottom of that coal mine all day. Finally, at the end of the shift, they brought him home in a wheelbarrow.

They dumped him on the back porch of his house and said to his wife, "Sorry, Phoebe, Teddy's dead." There was no Worker's Compensation. No insurance. And without Teddy, there was no income. At the tender age of eleven, my grandfather was the oldest child of four. The next day, he took his father's place as the breadwinner and went to work in the mine yard as a breaker boy. The family had to continue making some kind of income because they lived in a house owned by the coal company. They bought their groceries at the company store.

You may have heard the old Tennessee Ernie Ford song, "I owe my soul to company store." That was literally true for my grandad's family. For the next thirty years, my granddad worked in the coal mines in Pennsylvania. Eventually John L. Lewis organized miners from many states into a labor union called the United Mine Workers, and working conditions improved a little. Mr. Lewis was the patron saint of my family. He was a controversial man, but he helped make life better for many miners and their families.

I say all that to say I come from a blue-collar background, where unions were usually thought to be right and management was usually thought to be wrong. My granddad's guiding political philosophy was "If you don't know who to vote for in a political election, find out who big business is backing and vote the other way." That was the voting principle that was consistently applied throughout my growing up years. I grew up thinking that I would probably be a lawyer for labor unions. But things didn't turn out that way. Through a variety of providential circumstances, I ended up becoming a lawyer who primarily represented management.

In my career, I was involved in giving advice to, and conferring with, corporate management about some very thorny and difficult labor issues, like cut-backs and lay-offs. I would go into those meetings with mixed emotions because of my background in labor unions and my father's training of me, combined with my law school training. I realized truth usually laid somewhere between the union and the management positions. Unions are not always right, and management is not always wrong. Neither side has a monopoly on the truth, although they often act like they do. In the course of my life, I've met many people on both sides of the labor and management fence. I've also met people who were remarkably rich and others who were desperately poor. I've met men and women at the top of their game and others who were barely surviving at their lowest point. Regardless of their circumstances, labor, management, wealthy, poor, high or low, I've discovered a common theme that runs through each life. Character makes the difference.

In fact in all the cases I've handled over decades of my legal career, I found character can make the difference in the outcome of the case.

I defended a civil lawsuit many years ago involving the termination of seven public employees. I represented the people who made the decision to fire them. I thought we had a strong case, but during the course of one court hearing, my client told a whopping lie. He had done something wrong and he wouldn't own up to it, even to me in private. The worst of it came out when a tape recording was produced proving conclusively this public official was lying through his teeth. I was depressed and disappointed. Here was a person in whom the public reposed confidence, and he not only lied, he lied repeatedly, shamelessly, and even to his own lawyer! Shortly afterward he was voted out of office.

From my exposure to labor/management disputes and my involvement in lawsuits, I have learned that of all the many circumstances, quirks, and events that seem to determine a case— or a person's destiny– character determines success. This is true both in a person's professional life and in their personal life.

I learned this lesson early on. Before I went to law school I considered becoming a minister. That kind of creates a problem when your last name is Priest because people don't know what to call you. Are you Preacher Priest, Father Priest, Pastor Priest? I eventually switched my major in college from pre-ministerial to pre-law, but during this transition time, I was still doing some preaching on the side. One Sunday I preached in a little country church for a very small crowd.

Afterward a frail, wizened lady came up to me and said, "Mr. Priest, that was a wonderful sermon. You're going to make a wonderful minister."

I said, "Well thank you, ma'am, but I'm going to be a lawyer." She looked at me sadly with a dropped jaw as she said in a very disappointed voice, "Why are you going the other way?" Ever since then, I've tried to convince people I really didn't go the other way. In fact, years after graduating law school, I resumed my ministerial studies and was ordained as a minister in my denomination. I guess I've come full circle.

But whether I'm wearing my lawyer's hat or my minister's hat, I have found it's not the people who are the smartest, it's not the people who are the richest, it's not the people who are most innovative who enjoy long-term, true success in their personal and professional life. It's the people who have certain consistent character qualities and live a life of virtue regardless of uncertain circumstances faced.

I want to share with you about a man who exhibited character qualities that ultimately made him a success although his path was marked by a number of disappointments and unfairness. I don't know his last name, but his first name was Joseph and he's mentioned in the Old Testament book of Genesis. Joseph was a guy who may be like some of you. He faced a lot of uncertainty in his life, a lot of ups and downs. In fact, if you graphed out Joseph's life, it would look like this:

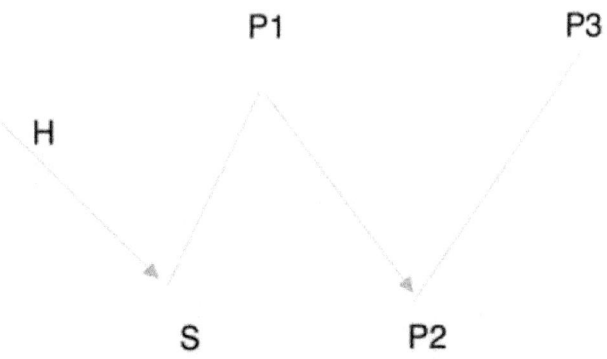

Joseph started out in childhood leading a charmed life as his father's favorite son at home (H). He had plenty of peaks and valleys after that. He was sold into slavery by his brothers (S). He rose through the ranks of slaves and became the number two person in the household of the powerful Egyptian named Potiphar (P1). But Potiphar's wife falsely accused Joseph of rape and had him thrown into prison (P2) where he served the head jailor faithfully and became a seemingly forgotten servant to everyone in the jail. Finally an opportunity arose for him to interpret the dream of the most powerful man in Egypt—the Pharaoh! Joseph impressed Pharaoh so much, he was made the number two man in the entire kingdom of Egypt (P3). But look how he got to his lofty position. Eventually he was very, very successful in both his professional and personal life, but it wasn't a steady climb to the top like a lot of us think successful people experience. It was a hard road of ups and downs.

Joseph's life was very uncertain because of circumstances beyond his control. People abused him, misused him, forgot him, and abandoned him. Or so it seemed. In reality Joseph's circumstances were in the hands of the God of providence, who had planted seeds of character in Joseph that ripened into the fruit of virtue. Between those character qualities and God's providential sovereignty, Joseph's life eventually became successful in the fullest sense of the word. Let's examine four character qualities that marked Joseph's life on the HIGHway to success!

Chapter Two: Honor

Showing respect to people even when they may not deserve it

If you've ever cracked open the Old Testament book of Genesis, it's hard to miss Joseph. His story occupies nearly half the first book of the Old Testament. The Genesis account, found in chapters 37 through 50, relates the story of a man named Jacob who had twelve sons, one of whom was our hero, Joseph. If you had wanted to find Joseph in those days, you could not have looked him up in the phone book. He didn't have a last name. But Joseph is a person well-worth finding.

When the story opens, we find Joseph near the bottom of the heap—the next to youngest in a group of twelve brothers. You would think being that far down in the food chain would have given Joseph an inferiority complex. But Joseph had the distinction of being the son his father loved the very most.

I don't know how many of you were the favorite child. I, of course, was. At least that's what I keep telling my sister. Generally you have certain perks when you're the favorite child, and Joseph got those perks. He had love lavished upon him by his daddy. I'm sure he occupied a seat of honor at the supper table. He had a special garment stitched by his father–the famous coat of many colors. No question about it, old Jacob played favorites, and Joseph was clearly his favorite.

Unfortunately those perks brought some downside risks. Even though he was beloved by his father and he had this wonderful, colorful coat, Joseph was very unpopular with his brothers. Fact is they were downright bitter with jealousy over Joseph. Now I'm not going to ask for a show of hands on how many of you had jealous brothers and sisters, but you probably had some siblings that weren't so crazy about you at one time or another. Maybe they picked on you or spoke badly about you. That was Joseph's situation. In his family, he was caught between a rock and a hard spot—the rock of his father's love and the hard spot of his brothers' jealousy.

When you read Genesis chapter 37, it's easy to understand why the brothers weren't that crazy about Joseph. Joseph kept having dreams where he always came out on top and the brothers (and his parents) took a back seat. Joseph made his brothers his enemies by bragging about his dreams at the breakfast table.

You can picture them talking at breakfast over a bowl of Wheaties, can't you?

Joseph would say, "Hey! I had a dream last night, guys. I dreamed there were all these sheaves of grain out in the field, and my sheave was standing up, and all of your sheaves were bowing down." The brothers would all grumble and throw food at Joseph and run him out of the kitchen. At least that's how I picture it. I don't have a doctorate in family counseling, but that's not the kind of dream I would share with my brothers, especially older, bigger brothers.

Joseph was one of those little kids that just didn't know enough to quit.

He had another dream, and once again, over a bowl of Ovaltine this time, he told his brothers, "I dreamed that the moon and the stars and the sun all bowed down and worshiped me."

The brothers kind of looked around at one another as they bent over their breakfast cereal and under their breath grumbled, "We're going to get this guy when he least expects it." And sure enough, they did.

Leadership Is an Inside Job

One day Joseph was at home while his older brothers were a long way away, working over on the other side of the family farm. I think he must have been so favored by his father that Joseph was exempted from chores. His brothers had been gone for several days, and Dad was worried, so he sent Joseph to check on the welfare of his brothers. Joseph traveled for several days and finally caught up with his brothers and the herd.

The brothers saw Joseph coming from a long way off, said, "Here comes the dreamer. Now is our chance. Let's get this dreamer boy and kill him."

One of the older brothers said, "I've got a better idea. Let's not kill him. Let's sell him into slavery and then we'll make some money and be rid of him." Talk about maximizing innovative creativity!

So quick as you like, they grabbed him, stripped off his colorful robe, and dropped him in a dried up well. Pretty soon a caravan of merchants passed by on the way to Egypt. and the brothers sold Joseph into slavery.

Then they dipped the coat in goat blood and brought Joseph's coat to their dad and said, "Dad, there wasn't any name label on this coat like we all have when go off to summer camp, but do you think this could be Joseph's coat?" Of course Jacob recognized the coat and jumped to the conclusion that Joseph had been attacked by an animal out in the wild and was dead. The old man cried and cried and could not be consoled, thinking his favorite boy was killed.

Well that is a pretty dirty trick to play on both Joseph and the dad. You can tell a lot about the brothers from this story–they're cold and heartless and selfish, and I think Joseph had every reason to distrust these guys, even before they did these despicable things. Despite that

Joseph exhibited one of the first character qualities absolutely essential for success in your personal and professional life, and that is honor.

The first H on the H*I*G*H*way to Success" stands for honor. Honor is showing respect and dignity, even to those who don't seem to deserve it. Joseph showed honor even to his loutish brothers, who didn't deserve it by going out and checking on their welfare when he would probably have rather stayed home. He had no reason to go and lots of reasons not to want to see if his brothers were doing alright.

He might have said, "Dad, those guys are always picking on me because I'm the younger brother. They don't like me because I have those dreams. Why don't you send young Benjamin to go? They kind of like him. He's the runt of the litter."

Joseph could have come up with a million excuses. But the Old Testament story tells us that he immediately did what his father asked him. He showed honor and respect to his father by obeying him and doing something he didn't want to do. And he also showed honor and respect to his brothers, despite the fact they didn't deserve it.

Now it's true, Joseph wasn't perfect in showing honor. When he was bragging about his dreams to the brothers, he was not honoring them. When he did it again, he was doubling down on his immaturity and foolishness. In fact it was likely this conduct, along with his dad's favoritism, got him in trouble with his brothers in the first place. Even though Joseph wasn't perfect, he still showed honor by obeying his father and checking on the welfare of his brothers.

I won't ask for a show of hands, but I'm wondering if there are any people in your life who don't deserve honor and respect to whom you should give it Are there people who have made fun of you? Dumped on you? Stripped you of something important and sold you out? Yeah. There's lots of folks out there like that. As a lawyer, I ran into them every day. Believe it or not, I had people during my law career who were not that friendly to me. The whole basis of courts is called the adversarial system. Well they don't call it "adversarial" for nothing. I had many adversaries. While most lawyers try to be adversaries in a professional manner, it doesn't always work that way.

When I was practicing law, I had to deal with a government agency lawyer who was not particularly friendly. Even in that situation, I tried to show respect and honor to that individual, as best I could, even when I didn't feel like it and even when the person didn't deserve it. I'd like to say he finally came around and showed respect and honor back. But he didn't.

Showing honor and respect to those around you, even when they don't deserve it, will distinguish you as a person of excellence. It applies in the work world, but it applies equally in your personal or family life. Do you show honor to those in your family, to your spouse, your parents, your children? Do you respect them even when you disagree with them? Do you show them kindnesses even when they haven't been to kind to you?

I have two children who are grown and married now, Amanda and Spence. When they were little, I had what I thought was a great disciplinary technique. I came up with a punishment known as "the flick." If the kids were misbehaving or acting up, I would just reach over and give them a little flick on the head or sometimes on the outside of their ear. If Spence was acting up, I'd give him a little flick on the ear. When Amanda was acting up, I'd give her a little flick in the head.

`Then one day I was reading a book by Gary Smalley who said he used to use the same technique on his kids until one day at a restaurant when he flicked his son, the little guy said, "Ow, Dad, that hurts. I don't like it when you flick me."

Smalley's daughter piped up and said, "I don't like it when you do it to me either." Smalley said his wife didn't say anything because he had never flicked her. Smart man. Smalley said he suddenly realized when he flicked his kids in public, he was showing dishonor toward them, and he decided right then to stop doing that.

Smalley's discussion really hit home with me, and I realized I was disrespecting my kids, too. So I began looking for ways to administer discipline in a way that didn't degrade them. That doesn't mean I stopped disciplining them or reprimanding them, even in public, when they needed it. But I tried to weave discipline in their lives in a way that still showed them honor.

It's not always easy. You know in your life, it's not easy to show honor to people who don't deserve it.

Showing honor doesn't mean you genuflect when you see them and say, "All hail, oh, great one," but it means that you treat them with courtesy and respect.

Or as I'd tell my kids when they were young, "You need to treat your brother and sister at least as good as you treat a total stranger." Often we treat total strangers with more respect and honor than we treat our own family members.

Joseph showed his brothers honor even when, and even though, they didn't deserve it. By doing so, he displayed for us the first character quality for success: HONOR.

Honor is showing respect and giving service to everyone, even to those who may not deserve it

Chapter Three: Integrity

Doing the right thing even when nobody is watching

Well back to the story. Joseph's in the pit. His brothers drag him up. They sell him into slavery. Off he goes to the land of Egypt where he doesn't know anyone, doesn't speak the language, and is sold to the highest bidder. Sounds like some summer jobs I've had. But Joseph's situation was much worse. He was sold as a slave to a guy named Potiphar, who was the chief bodyguard for the Pharaoh of Egypt. Joseph is on the lowest rung on the social ladder: he's an immigrant, an illegal alien, working without compensation or any communication with home. Despite this adversity, he displays character. He begins to be consistent every day in the quality of his work and loyalty to his boss. Little by little, Potiphar begins to take notice of this guy.

He says, "Hey, when I entrust Joseph with something, it gets done. It's timely completed. There's zero defects. I'm going to give this guy more responsibility!" Potiphar begins to load him up with more and more authority, and Potiphar realizes everything he gives to Joseph, God honors and blesses, and Joseph has success. He makes Potiphar look good!

Joseph basically, the slave boy from another country, is running the house of the bodyguard of the Pharaoh. Pretty soon the only thing that Potiphar has withheld from Joseph in the entire household is his wife. Now Potiphar's wife is an interesting character. Personally I've never run into a woman like this. She chased Joseph all over the house because Joseph was handsome. Maybe that's why I've never run into a woman like this. We don't know her name, but we know her seductions.

Day after day she would consistently say to Joseph, "Come sleep with me." I've always thought that's an interesting phrase. It's not the sleeping that gets people in trouble, it's what happens before the sleeping. But anyway she's grabbing Joseph and she's trying to seduce him, and Joseph refused.

"No, I'm not going to do that."

It really was the first recorded incident of sexual harassment in the workplace.

Joseph keeps rejecting her, and this seems to make him more irresistible to her. She keeps after him every day. I imagine it was tough to resist a persistent and insistent woman who is clearly making herself available. Finally she physically grabs Joseph by the coat, and with her most enticing smile and voice, pleads with him to go to bed with her. What does Joseph do? He runs! He leaves in such a hurry, he pulls out of the coat she's grabbing, leaving it in her grasp. You'll notice this guy keeps losing coats. First the coat of many colors and now this one. It's just like me in kindergarten. I was always losing my coats.

Joseph runs, out but before he does, he says, "How could I do such a great sin against my God and my master, Potiphar?" He bolts out the door leaving temptation –and his coat–behind.

The coat. You know where that was. In the hand of the spurned woman. Now it is Exhibit A in the case of *Potiphar vs. Joseph*, a case of alleged attempted rape.

Unfortunately for Joseph, I was not there to represent him. I'm sure I would have gotten the case dismissed. But Joseph had no defense attorney, and before you could say "lost my coat," Joseph found himself in prison convicted, without a trial, on false charges of attempted rape. Now think about this. It reminds me of a phrase a friend of mine told me one time. "No good deed goes unpunished." Joseph did something very good. He showed the second characteristic of success, integrity. He did what he was supposed to do in resisting temptation. Integrity is defined as what you do when no one is watching. He could have had a roll in the hay with Potiphar's wife. Maybe nobody would have found out. But he would have known. The person of integrity does consistently what they ought to do, regardless of who's watching.

And his reward for doing the right thing? Prison.

Now it wouldn't take me too long to figure out integrity doesn't pay. Joseph does the right thing and finds himself in the pits again. Remember? He's doing pretty well in the family. Does the right thing in checking on this brothers, and his reward was to be thrown in a pit and sold into slavery. He gets to Potiphar's house and again does the right thing, enjoys temporary success but then gets convicted on a bum rap, and he's down in jail again.

Kind of reminds me of a story I read the other day in the paper about a husband and a wife. This guy decided he didn't like his wife very much, so he threw her off a high balcony. She was pretty quick though. She grabbed onto the railing. So he got a hammer and began hitting her fingers. Fortunately below her on the patio, there was a guy that saw what was going on, and just as the husband smashed the last of his wife's fingers with the hammer, the passerby caught her as she fell.

When the husband was prosecuted for his dirty deed, the wife testified—unbelievably–on her husband's behalf, saying, "Oh, I don't think he really meant anything by it."

Wow.

Well that was kind of like what happened to Joseph. Potiphar's wife hit his fingers with a hammer and he found himself in a pit again, despite the fact he displayed integrity. His reward for his exemplary behavior was to be thrown in jail. No good deed goes unpunished.

Despite the opportunity to cheat with his boss's wife, Joseph showed integrity—doing the right thing, even when nobody was watching. Fortunately his story doesn't end there.

Chapter Four: Grace

Showing concern for others when you'd rather be talking about your own problems

If I had been Joseph, unjustly jailed, you know how I would have spent my time? Writing legal briefs. Trying to get out of there. I would have complained to every person who would lend me an ear and some that wouldn't listen about what a bum rap I got.

I'd say, "Hey. You think you've got problems? Listen to me. I'll tell you. This is a bum rap. It started out with my brothers." And I'd tell them the whole story.

But Joseph didn't do that. He showed the third character quality of success, grace. Grace is showing concern for others when you'd rather be talking about your own problems.

The Old Testament tells us Joseph served others in jail, and his service was noticed. Like in Potiphar's house, the head jailer learned pretty quickly and thought, hey. This Joseph guy has the golden touch. Whatever he does succeeds. I'm going to entrust more work to him. The jailer began giving Joseph more responsibilities, and success followed.

Pretty soon Joseph was in charge of the entire jail and the jailer was looking good. Remember the same thing that happened at Potiphar's house. Joseph would go from cell to cell. One day he found a couple of guys with long faces, not literally but figuratively. They were depressed over confusing dreams they each had.

Instead of saying, "Hey! What's your problem? You think you've got problems? Listen to my story," Joseph said, "What's was your dream? God will help me interpret it." The inmates told him their dreams, and to make a long story short, Joseph gave an interpretation to each.

One man, Joseph predicted, was going to die. But the other fellow, the wine taster for the Pharoh, received better news.

"You will be restored to the right hand of the Pharaoh. And when you get there, don't forget me. Put in a good word to the Pharaoh for me."

In doing this, Joseph shows grace, which is the ability to show concern for other people's problems when you'd rather be talking about your own. Once again Joseph is showing his character. And what's his reward? Does the man who is set free put in a good word with Pharoh? Nope. The guy he helped promptly forgot him. Joseph ends up staying in jail for several more years. More good deeds punished.

If I had been an Executive Coach for Joseph, I would have said, "Well, Joseph, let's look at your pattern here. You show honor to those who don't deserve it, and you get thrown in the pit. You show integrity in the midst of sexual temptation, and you get thrown in jail. You show grace to people in a difficult circumstance when you'd rather be talking about your own problems, and for your reward, you remain locked in jail. Joseph, how's that working for you? Maybe you ought to try lying, cheating, and stealing. It couldn't be worse."

But Joseph wouldn't have listened to that kind of advice. He continued to consistently display those character qualities of honor, integrity, and grace. Finally, one day years later, this man that got out of jail remembered Joseph.

The Pharaoh had a bad dream, a really weird one. You've probably had weird dreams. Sometimes when I wake up, I try to relate them to my wife, but often I can't remember half of it. But Pharaoh remembered his dream. The whole thing. It was about seven fat cows. The fat cows were grazing, and along came seven skinny cows. The skinny cows ate up the fat cows.

Whoa. Weird dream.

That's the kind of dream that most dairy farmers don't want to have. Pharaoh was troubled by it, too, and he didn't know what to do. Finally the servant of Pharaoh who was in jail with Joseph had an a-ha moment and remembered him.

"Oh. Hey. I remember there was a guy in jail who helped me and interpreted my dream. He could probably help you, Pharaoh."

They brought Joseph up out of jail, and he commenced to interpreting the dream.

Joseph said, "I can tell you what that dream means. The nation is going to have seven years of plenty. That's what the seven fat cows represent. You're going to have lots and lots of crops. But then you're going to have seven years of famine. That's what the skinny cows represent. You need to be prepared for the famine. Think ahead. Plan ahead. Store up during the good years, so you'll be prepared in the lean years. If I were you, Pharaoh, I would put somebody in charge who knows what they're doing during the seven years of plenty, so you're ready for the seven years of want." Joseph got ready to return to jail, but Pharaoh said, "Wait a minute. You da man." It's right there in the Bible. "You da man. Who else could I put in charge that would be better than you?"
Pharaoh put a ring of authority on Joseph's finger.

He gave Joseph a beautiful robe, even better than the coat of many colors, and Pharaoh said, "I put you in charge of everything. You are second only to me."

Wow. Did Joseph finally get his reward? Yeah. Finally. But was it a straight line trajectory upward? No. Remember the graph? Joseph started out pretty good, then he went to the pit. Literally. Then he succeeds in Potiphar's household, and his reward was to be thrown in jail. He's left in jail for a long time but finally gets his chance and gets out. As the number two official for Pharaoh, he successfully prepared for and navigated the famine. Notice again Joseph did not experience a smooth consistent upward path to the top. There were lots of ups and downs along the way. But through it all, Joseph lived a life of values, regardless of his circumstances.

Chapter 5 Humility

Recognizing there is a God and you are not Him

Here's the great irony. There finally was some justice for Joseph. His brothers, who lived in another other country, had to come to him and beg for food, Some say there is no justice. Ha!

I heard a story about justice some years ago. True story. There was a federal judge who was trying to pull into the federal courthouse parking lot one morning. It was one of those entrances where the gates come up, and the judge couldn't get in because a car in front didn't have the access code or the money to raise the gate. The judge was going to be late to a criminal sentencing hearing, so he tapped lightly on his horn to encourage the guy in the first car to move. But the guy in front leans out of the window and flips off the federal judge. Of course the guy with the crude gesture didn't know he was flipping off a federal judge.

Finally both the front car and the judge get in. The judge sprints upstairs, puts his robe on, and heads out to the courtroom for the criminal sentencing. Guess who the criminal defendant was. Right. The guy who flipped him off.

The judge later reportedly said, "And some people say there is no justice."

The same thought must have gone through Joseph's mind. Here come his brothers begging for food. They don't recognize him. Ultimately he helps them. He gives food to them. He welcomes them with open arms. He helps them set up households in Egypt. They have everything they need.

Joseph's dad is still alive. Remember him? The man who gave Joseph the coat of many colors. Dad comes down to Egypt, and

71

he weeps and hugs Joseph. It's a great family reunion. For several years, things rock on very nicely. All the family is together.

But then Dad dies. The brothers (except Joseph) get together the same brothers who got together around the pit — and they're still conspiring. They haven't really changed.

They said, "You know, Joseph is in charge and he's the big man on campus and he's powerful, and Dad's dead, and now we don't have a buffer. We better come up with some kind of story to make sure that Joseph doesn't hurt us."

So they go to Joseph and they lie.

They say, "Joseph, we forgot to mention this. Just before Dad died, he said to pass this message along to you. 'Please be kind to your brothers and forgive them all their many trespasses.'" Joseph probably knew this was a lie, but instead of calling them out, he has a memorable talk with them in which he forgives them.

If it were me, I would have said, "Dad didn't say that. I know my father wouldn't have said something like that. You guys are still the same conniving slime balls you were when you threw me in the pit. And now you're going to get your comeuppance." That's what I would have said. Instead Joseph says, "Am I in God's place? You meant it for evil, but God meant it for good, to bring about all that you see around you." Wow. Look at those words. "Am I in God's place?" He showed our final character quality on the HIGH-way of success: humility.

Joseph was a very powerful guy. He was the number two man, the COO of Egypt. Yet instead of throwing his weight around and retaliating against his conniving brothers, he recognizes he is not God and he is not in God's place.

I had a friend back in college who was from Nigeria, Edwin Obieke. Sometimes people would tease Edwin and do funny things to him, just joking around, but I didn't like it.

I said, "Edwin, does that ever make you mad?"

Edwin, ever polite, said, "Oh, no, Mr. Priest. I know the Bible says, 'Vengeance is mine, I will repay, sayeth the Lord.' But sometimes I let the Lord use me as an instrument of His wrath."

But Joseph wasn't like that. He didn't let the Lord use him as an instrument of wrath. He recognized the two foundational truths of human enlightenment.

1. There is a God.
2. You are not Him.

Wouldn't it be good if everybody knew that?

If you look at the life of Joseph and consider any one moment of his life, you might be tempted to think, man, this guy is doing the right things, but he's not getting rewarded. He needs to look out for himself and not be so concerned about his values.

- He showed honor to his brothers and father, but he ended up in the pit.
- He showed integrity in the midst of sexual temptation, but he ended up in jail.
- He showed grace to people in prison, but they forget about him.
- He showed humility when he could have showed revenge.

What is it about this guy?

Joseph recognized what hopefully we all recognize: success is not defined by where you are on the corporate ladder, or by what you do, or how much money you take home. True success in your personal life and professional life is defined by the character qualities that you cultivate and which define you.

You are capable of cultivating these character qualities.

You may think, oh, man. If I were in the situations Joseph faced, I could never have done what he did. I don't have that kind of character.

But you do.

Has there never been a time in your life you've shown at least a little integrity? Sure there has. Has there ever been a time you've shown honor to somebody who didn't deserve it? I'll bet so. Or grace? Have you helped someone when you'd rather have talked about your own problems? Or humility by not throwing your weight around, even though you could have?

At some point you have displayed all of these character qualities. Maybe in small measure, but you've done it at some point in your life. You have the seeds of character and success waiting to blossom within you. I believe you can be a person of honor, a person of integrity, a person who displays grace and humility. Make the choice to cultivate those character qualities, and you'll find success in your professional and your personal life.

PART 3:

An interview with Jim Priest

NM: Welcome to the Strata Leadership Show. This is your host, Dr. Nathan Mellor. Today we have a dear friend of mine, Jim Priest, who is joining our show. Jim is someone who I think the world of, and we have spent a lot of time together hiking in different national parks throughout the country. Jim is the president and CEO at Goodwill Industries of Central Oklahoma. If you look him up on LinkedIn, which I would suggest that you should, Jim is someone who is constantly contributing meaningful things on social media. Jim is someone who would refer to himself as a people developer, and I couldn't agree more. Jim, welcome to the show.

JP: It is great to be here, Nathan. Thank you for the invitation.

NM: Jim is somebody who cares deeply about people and ideas. One of the reasons that I have admired him is because of his ability to connect people. Matter of fact, we really have hiked a lot of miles together, and if you have hiked very much, you know that people give each other trail names. And the trail name that I gave Jim Priest a few years ago is the trail name "The Bridge." And the reason I gave him that title is because I have never seen someone who has the ability to create a bridge between different groups. He is the kind of person that even if you disagree with him, you listen to him because he would listen to you if he disagreed with you. I have really enjoyed watching Jim's career. His background is in non-profit executive leadership and also in law. He has been a columnist for our state's largest newspaper for a number of years. And he is someone who is always trying to connect people and ideas. When you look at the idea of being a leader, Jim, who is someone, if you could think of people who have made an impact on you as a leader, who would be someone you say that person helped shape who I am today?

JP: Two people come immediately to mind. One that I know personally and one that I just watched and read and had the good fortune to meet. The person that I knew personally and lived with is my dad. He was a leader in some arenas of his life. And he was kind of a quiet, backbench guy in other areas. He was involved in the labor movement. He was a union leader. He was a leader in our Boy Scout group and he was a leader in our church. But he wasn't engaged in what I would call community agencies or United Way or anything like that. He was kind of selective about it. But he shaped me in so many ways. He is undoubtedly the single greatest influence in my life, and I have written a lot about him.

The person that I didn't know personally, although I have met on a couple of occasions, but who shaped me a lot in my attitudes is Zig Ziglar. Zig has written prolifically and has done a lot of recordings. I have listened to him speak live on several occasions. I have a picture of the two of us standing together, like most groupies, and it is one of my prized possessions. In the photo, I am looking very young and slender, and he is looking like Zig, with a big smile. One of my proudest moments was when I learned Zig had quoted me in one of his books on

success. Those two influential people, one was up close and personal and the other was more distant, have probably influenced me the greatest.

NM: I appreciate both of those examples. I know how much you loved your dad while he was here with us and how much you love him now as he is gone. And I love hearing about people who have influenced people, and they may not have had a personal relationship, but they were still connected. I do appreciate both of those examples. And I, too, remember listening to Zig Ziglar tapes. He had a way of connecting and inspiring and just making you feel like you could do it, and I appreciate that very much. You grew up in the northeast and you graduated from Syracuse Law School back in 1980. Right now in this interview, you are sitting at your office in Goodwill Industries, and I am assuming that when you walked across the stage in 1980 and got that law degree, you were not imagining that in some point in the future you would be leading this huge enterprise of Goodwill Industries. How did you get to where you are now? If I were having this version of you talking to the version of you that just walked across the stage, what advice would you give that young lawyer about the future that was ahead?

JP: Well, just to briefly sketch, I left home after graduating Syracuse Law School in Upstate New York, which is my hometown, because I had married a Texas girl who encouraged me to live somewhere it wasn't winter nine months of the year. She wanted to move out west or southwest, so we came to Oklahoma City, and I was fortunate to get a job with a relatively small law firm

of about ten lawyers. It grew to a law firm of about seventy-five lawyers. I was there for twenty-five years and practiced employment law, civil rights, and constitutional law. I did a lot of trial work, which I thought, when I was young, was what all lawyers did. When I was young, I probably wanted to became a lawyer because it looked cool on TV, but when I grew older, I understood lawyers help people solve problems, and that's what ultimately motivated me. I did a lot of trial work and learned so much at the law firm. Later I went on and practiced law in a couple of different firms. I knew I wanted to have an impact in a bigger way than helping people through legal problems. So I ran for Oklahoma Attorney General in 2010 and I lost that race. I'm glad I ran, and I wish I had won, but many of the good things in my life would not have happened had I won.

Losing that race turned out to be a pivot point in my life. I ended up getting in the non-profit arena after that, first working for a small non-profit that dealt with substance abuse issues. Then I went to a non-profit called Sunbeam Family Services that did a variety of social services. Then I went to Goodwill Industries of Central Oklahoma where I serve today.

I think to your second question, what advice would I give the young Jim Priest walking across the stage? I think part of what I would tell him is to be relentlessly purposeful. That is a phrase a friend of mine uses when he talks about God.

He says, "God is relentlessly purposeful in our lives," and I think we have to be intentional about being purposeful. It sounds a little redundant, but so much of life just comes at us. We think, I guess I need to get married. Keep an eye out for a woman who will be faithful and true, pretty, kind to me, good to my kids. Someday we will have kids, and then I will progress, and maybe I will become a partner in a law firm.

A lot of that just happens because stuff is thrown at us or opportunities happen our way rather than us just sitting down and saying, "This is where I would like my life to end up."

I remember talking to a senior partner one time who was a very accomplished trial lawyer. I asked him, "How did you decide to get into what you are doing?"

He paused for a minute and said, "Well it just sort of happened." I remember thinking, even at that early stage of my career, that I didn't want that to be my story. I got into this, and it just sort of happened. I wanted to intentionally go somewhere and do something.

I began to apply that principle to different areas of my life, including being a dad, being a husband. That is the advice I think I would give the young Jim Priest. Just think about being intentionally purposeful in every area of your life.

NM: I smiled when you gave that description because it is one of those classic things that a leader would say. Don't waste your life and know where you want to go. Be purposeful. Be intentional. And I love what you are saying. I find it interesting because a lot of leaders think that people think that way when the reality is that they really don't. What point in your life did you realize that you were a leader that you could help influence how other people thought about themselves and their world and that was a way that you might be able to serve people?

JP: I had a very bad leadership experience in the sixth-grade. That was probably the first time that I thought I would like to be a leader. Of course you can't remember exactly what you were thinking back in the sixth-grade, but I think my idea of leadership was bossing people around. In the sixth-grade, you could be a crossing guard and the way they organized it, they would have an elected captain and a lieutenant and then all of the crossing guards would report to them. The crossing guards that were just crossing guards would be assigned to a post, some intersection, to make sure kids got across the streets safely on the way to school. Then the captain and lieutenant were in charge of making sure that people were at their post and filling in when somebody didn't show up and that sort of thing. We had the election, and all the crossing guards voted for who they wanted to be captain and who they wanted to be lieutenant. Of course I wanted to be the captain, but I came in second. I lost that election. I was voted lieutenant. A fellow student named Linda Waffle was elected captain. I later found out it was because there were more girls than boys among the crossing guards, and all the girls voted for Linda and all the guys voted for me. At the end of that time, I thought I had done a good job.

But I remember talking to a friend of mine named Buddy Milburg after we were finished with patrol duty, and I must have said something that made him mad because he just kind of punched his finger into my chest and said, "Nobody liked you anyway as lieutenant of the crossing guards because you were always bossing people around." Wow! I was stunned. I didn't get that sense at all from anybody, but I think he was probably right. I probably did boss people around and I didn't think about the now classic expression of being a servant leader. I had the cool red badge. I was the lieutenant. And even though I wasn't the captain, I was better than the crossing guards and I was all about the pecking order. So that's when I realized I was a leader but not a good one.

NM: I appreciate that example.

JP: That experience helped me recognize, it was more Buddy's rebuke of me that I needed to hear, that really got me thinking there is more to this leadership thing than just bossing people around.

NM: I am assuming Buddy the sixth grader or seventh grader, whatever he was at the time, may have been exaggerating a little bit. But that feeling of having someone say that to you, and it cuts so deep, is a feeling that all leaders know. It is one of those very distinct realities of being a leader that even if you have the right motives or whatever you put yourself out there to serve other people and you wanted to be a good leader. When you find out that people didn't feel that way about you, it is always hurtful. So we fast forward from that moment to running for office. Same idea. I am willing to put myself out there for whatever reason. I am willing to allow myself to be voted on in a system that might be fair or it might not be, whatever it may be. Why are you willing to put yourself in the line of fire, so to speak, to be open to rejection in moments like those? Why are you willing to endure that pain?

JP: I think it is rooted in something my dad told me one time. This was probably after I had set my sights on going to law school.

He said, "Don't ever forget where you came from." I grew up in a lower middle-class family, but my dad grew up in a very poor family. My grandpa was a coal miner in Pennsylvania, and it was a very hand to mouth existence. I knew that I came from people of great need and poverty. So I made it a goal to try and help vulnerable people because I was in the position where I could do some things, and you always have to be careful because you don't want to come across as "Hey, there is a vulnerable person, and I know what they need and I am going to give them five dollars." Or "I am going to meet their needs" without really listening well to what their needs are or what they perceive their needs to be. That was my theme when I campaigned for attorney general. I felt like it was the obligation and the responsibility of the attorney general for any state and the state of Oklahoma to safeguard vulnerable people. Not to stick up for big companies. To be the lawyer for the people. To stand up and speak for those who have no voice. I represented lots of different kinds of people through my law career, but I got the most satisfaction representing people who had no voice for themselves.

NM: That is one of the reasons that I love and admire you because I would say that whether you had been an elected official or not, you have pursued that mission faithfully. I look at the role that you are in now, that is the role that I am so happy that you are in, but even this role that you have now is not unique in the sense of these are the types of things that you have been trying to connect with and promote and be a part of since as long as I have known you. Looking at Goodwill, I was really amazed by the scale of the good work that is being done by Goodwill. Can you tell us a little bit about Goodwill and just a description of the scale of it and what you are accomplishing through it?

JP: I think everyone is familiar with Goodwill Thrift Stores. So the phrase that I have been trying to use more in my talking about what we do is "We are more than a store. We are a store and much more." Our mission statement is to help people overcome challenges to employment and transform lives through the power of work. So much of our lives are spent at work, and we have such a great opportunity in work, particularly those of us that have the opportunity to influence culture. We have the opportunity to really transform people's lives. It is not just giving them a source of income, which is certainly a good part of that and an important part of it, but all of us derive a lot of self-worth from our work. Through work we have the opportunity to meet people's needs. That is what Goodwill does.

In our stores here in central Oklahoma, we have about 750 employees and about a thirty-two-million-dollar budget in 2020. We employ a lot of people in our stores but not only do we employ them, we provide wrap around services to those who need them. We have a number of people who are coming out of justice system involvement; we are a second chance employer. Most of these people need to get their foot on the first rung of

the ladder after they get out of prison. That person has a lot of needs not just for income, although certainly income is one. They may be struggling with family issues or psychological issues, emotional issues, substance use, or housing issues. We began a program here called Begin at Home where we provide wrap around services for those who work in our stores.

Then we have a variety of other programs for folks that are not involved as Goodwill employees. We provide services to homeless veterans. In fact this last month we were able to house 100 homeless vets in thirty days. We just did a big blitz and tried to get homeless vets off the street and into temporary housing where we could transition them into permanent housing. We are also involved helping folks perform community service that has been mandated by the courts, and sometimes they want to transition to permanent employment with us. We do a lot of job opportunity seeking for folks. Sometimes they end up at Goodwill, but sometimes we help them find jobs elsewhere. We provide job training. We have the Goodwill Career Pathway Institute, an accredited educational program, where we provide hard side and soft side skills to people. Some of them need just basic stuff, like how to interview for a job. How do I fill out an online application? Some of them are the next level up. What is EQ, emotional intelligence, and why is that important in whatever job I have? So we have a broad array of services. I had a graphic artist recently put together a picture because I think better in pictures.

I said, "I am imagining a big building that Goodwill is housed in and it has different doors and windows representing the different services that we provide to the community. Here is what it looks like." I drew this awful drawing, kind of hand-scratched on a piece of paper and gave it to my graphic artist, and she made it into a beautiful picture that I think helps us understand better what we do.

NM: You know, it really is amazing all that you are doing. And how many stores are a part of your network?

JP: In central Oklahoma, we have twenty-five stores and eighteen independent donation centers. All of the stores have a donation center attached to them, but some places we have just a stand-alone donation center where people can come and give us used goods. Sometimes people give us their junk, and if that is mixed in there, then we dispose of it. One of the things we really try to do is to be good stewards and recycle. Very little goes to waste. We put very little of what we get into the trashcan. We either sell it in the store, or if it doesn't sell there, then it goes to our outlet store where we sell by the pound. If it doesn't sell there, then we sell it to salvage dealers. Many times tex-

tiles are purchased by people for pennies, but they are then sent overseas to folks who need clothing.

NM: It is an amazing system. The reputation of Goodwill is such a great reputation. For you as a leader, now you are leading twenty-five different locations, the eighteen stand-alone donation spots, you've got 750 or so employees, many of whom are transitioning to a new phase of their lives. This is a very complex system. There is so many constituents that are interacting with Goodwill at all times. When you think about the challenge of leading an organization with that kind of complexity, what would you say are some of the bigger challenges that you feel like a leader would face of taking something on like that?

JP: I think you are right in terms of the complexity. I think you have to simplify or at least make it as simple as possible without oversimplifying. So for me, the guiding principle that overarches lots of what I do, but all of what I think and plan is to create what I call an employee first culture. It is to communicate that our first priority is our employees. It's contrary to what is often the business mantra that the customer is always right. We try to follow the Southwest Airlines model of doing business. To say we are going to put primary consideration on how our decisions impact our employees. To have an employee first culture doesn't mean employees get everything they want. We don't pay the highest wages in the area. The work can be challenging. We don't coddle people. We have high expectations. But we communicate to them our belief that they can meet those ex-

pectations and then we constantly look for ways to create structures and policies and practices that serve our people rather than serve the company.

I will give just a quick illustration of this. We've had in the past some principles or policies in place that made life easier here at corporate. It was a uniform policy, and we administered to all the stores and all the employees. This made it easy to administer. It was good for us. But it really didn't take into consideration the uniqueness of each location and each person. We have a new vice-president of retail, Frank Holland, who has this employee first mindset also. Frank and I have just been sitting down and thinking about what we could do to really make this a place where we are serving our people rather than they are serving corporate convenience. It has been amazing in just the first sixty or ninety days that Frank arrived, he knew where to put his finger on the sore spots and tweak it and change it. We have people coming up to us that are newly energized and invigorated because we changed polices, but more importantly we communicated and valued the contribution of the people. Now it is like everything I look at and every book I read seems to be shouting that principle to me. I had purposefully sought out some of these books, but it is like the white Toyota principle. You don't pay attention to a white Toyota until you buy one and then you see them everywhere. Since we have been focused on employee first, it is coming up in almost every arena I see and read. I believe, like Southwest Airlines has proven, it will not only be good for our employees, but it will be good for our company. I think we will make more money, which will then

be reinvested into our mission. It will continue to compound interest as we invest in our people.

NM: I appreciate that so much from the standpoint of talking to corporate leaders who may not look at the world that way. You try to show them the data that goes behind it of taking care of your people is not just the better way to live, but it is also the better way to do business. I love hearing what you are getting at. I would say, let me give an example. I was having breakfast with a leader recently, and their company had to pull back on some of their benefits due to the downturn of the economy related to COVID-19. And this was a company that had taken great pride in how well they took care of their people, but they found themselves in the spot where they could not do everything that they wanted to do. This leader was just broken hearted about it. It wasn't because of the business model, they were broken hearted about it because that was what they had hoped to be able to do together. They had dreamed of how incredible it would be if we could provide this for our team members, if we could provide these things, if we could be more aggressive in this way. I found it fascinating because this was someone who was not doing that begrudgingly. That was the goal, that was the dream. I appreciate again where you are coming from on that of making it about the people. When you think about leadership on the bigger picture of just leaders overall, you think about the complexity of what is happening in culture, the volatility, what is happening in culture right now. What would you say would be the biggest challenge that you think leaders are facing today?

JP: I think it is relationship and not being purposeful and intentional about making sure that first of all the relationships are established, and secondly, continue to build them. I am reading a book, listening to it, an audio book as well, called, *Leaders Eat Last* by Simon Sinek. He talks about the dysfunction in Washington among Congress, the Judiciary, and the Executive branch. At the time, he wrote it was dysfunctional, and it is even worse now. He attributes much of it to the lack of relationship that was the result people in Congress not living in Washington, D.C. area but deciding, sometime in the nineties, they would live full-time in their home districts and commute into Washington.

They said, "We will have a shortened work week. We will come in on Tuesday morning and leave Thursday night." As a result, there is no relationship. They don't know the people in the opposite party. All they know is that they are against whatever the other person is for. They never go to the ball games with each other. They don't sit in the same church pew with them. They don't go to barbeques together. There is no basis for to have a relationship.

Whether you are a member of Congress or a leader of non-profit or for-profit operation, relationship is everything. It is how we truly impact lives. I can make policies and establish priorities for Goodwill, but our organization is in trouble if I don't have relationship with everybody. My senior staff probably more in-depth than anyone. But I need to connect in some way with everyone. That's why I send all our employees handwritten birthday and work anniversary cards. I try to make it a point

every week to go out to the stores and the donation centers. I walk the warehouse and regularly and informally talk to those who deliver mission services. I listen to people. I find out what they are worried about. What are they concerned about? What do they think we are doing right? It is a small relationship, it is not deep. I don't see these people frequently. But I am trying to establish this type of relationship with them so when I do a Friday video, every Friday, and send it out to everybody, they can say, "Oh, yeah! That guy came in to talk to me. I remember him." I have a little bit more connectivity with the folks that work at Goodwill that way.

NM: That is good. That is really good stuff. On the dual concern model, which shows how conflict can be predicted, you have the five different conflict styles of avoiding, yielding, competing, compromising, or collaborating. It is interesting that the greater the concern you have for someone else while also having great concern about your own outcome, it changes what options are available on the table. If I don't care about it, if I don't care about the other people that I am negotiating with, then I am going to avoid. I am not going to engage. If I care a lot about somebody else and I don't care about myself, I am going to yield most likely. If I care me and I don't care about you, then I am going to compete. That is what we are describing almost a narcissistic world view where it is all about me and you are in my way. When I think that way, the only way I can win is to compete. I am going to have to go head-to-head with you every time. But if I am concerned about me and concerned about you, even on a medium level, I can compromise.

But if I am really concerned about you and I am really concerned about me, then I can collaborate. I love your answer. One of the challenges is that it just takes time. So as a leader, how do you set aside time to be able to build those relationships?

JP: One of the things I do is I have a white board in my office. I love white boards. I try to keep the big rocks listed on there. What are the things that I need to be doing every week and not let emergencies of the day eat up my day? I have on my white board to visit locations every Friday. That's when I do the Friday video, to talk about what's going on, big picture, and to interview one of our employees for a couple minutes. You find out all kinds of stuff when you just walk around. I think the marines call it "eyeball leadership." You just get out there and you see what is going on and you talk to people and ask questions. You get great insights.

Not too long ago I had a funny experience. I was walking through this area that is between the warehouse and the outlet store. We have this big piece of machinery called a tipper. What it is supposed to do is take a piece of equipment that has a bunch of donated goods, usually textiles, and it tips them into another flat container on wheels that we can take out into the outlet store. This gentleman who was working in this area came up to me and he knew who I was from the videos.

He said, "Hey, I want to let you know about something. Come with me!" He just dragged me over to this tipping machine. I didn't even know at that point what a tipping machine was. I had walked by it before, but I had never paid attention to it.

He said, "This thing has been broken for about sixty days. We can't seem to get the manufacturer to come in and give us the part. It is slowing us down. We can't get our work done! Something needs to be done about this!"

I was like, "You are right. Yes, I am glad you stopped me." I started to stick my nose into what was going on and found out who the manufacturer was and made some phone calls. I told them what the urgency of the situation was and it got fixed, not as quickly as I wanted it to, but it got fixed. I don't know how long it would have taken to get that fixed if that guy hadn't stopped me and told me. He had to have the chutzpah to go up and tell the CEO something was wrong. Some people would be intimidated to do that. It was good on his part that he had the chutzpah to do that, and I am glad that I make it my practice to walk around like that.

NM: A great example of creating an opportunity for that communication. Wrapping up our time, I so appreciate being able to spend some time with you. Wrapping up our time, a couple of questions. One is what would you say is your favorite thing about leadership? The impact that you can made on other people's lives. What would you say is your favorite thing about leadership?

JP: My favorite thing is that I feel I can make a difference. I tell people that I tried to do some of the things I am doing now in creating an employee first culture at some of the law firms where I worked, but I had pretty dilute power and I didn't have much leverage to get things done. I could never quite get enough momentum going with these ideas to have them take root. I am able to do that now and I've got buy in. When you go home at the end of the day, you think, I made a difference. I moved that project a little bit forward. Somedays you don't move anything forward, and somedays you are going backward. I heard a story this morning about a lady who was helped through our Begin at Home program, and she is one of our employees who is a single mom with four kids living in a 900-square-foot apartment. She doesn't make a lot of money, and she was having some food scarcity issues, and she was in this apartment that wasn't very safe.

Through the Begin at Home program, we invite employees to raise their hand and say, "Hey! I need some help" in these non-work-related areas. One of our folks was able to go through an inventory of needs to see what she needed, and within three days we had found her a rental house ,which had a backyard that her kids could play in. The rent is going to be paid temporarily by another non-profit that we have a partnership with. We hooked her up with the food bank, a resource she was unaware of. We got her connected with free counseling. We have made a tremendous difference in this lady's life through the efforts of our employees and making available to them this program of Begin at Home. I am only partly responsible because I have told people it is a priority and we are going to fund it and let's get going. But other people have made it happen. But when I went home that night, I thought that single mom employee with four kids, her life is better because of some of the things we are doing here. That is what jazzes me about leadership.

NM: Love it. You know, you and I have had a chance to go to a few national parks together for our executive summit series that we have at Strata where we bring executives together for a few days to really contemplate where they are and where they want to go. It is a pretty amazing experience really. But if you had to recommend one national park to, if you said this was a national park that everyone has to see, what is one that you would recommend?

JP: Probably Grand Tetons. They are all just so breathtaking in their own respect. I remember being up there and the majesty, the quietness, the wildlife. So probably that one. My son, Spencer, who is thirty-four-years-old, a couple of years ago he hiked the Pacific Crest Trail from Mexico to Canada and he saw 2,400 miles of natural beauty.

NM: Wow.

JP: It was a transformational experience for him. I spent a little bit of time with him at Yosemite, and it was great. Just getting out in nature is not only a restful experience, but it ministers to your soul. And I think that is part of why God created the beauty of nature is to be restorative to us as well. Maybe that is another piece of advice that I would have given to young Jim Priest. Get out in nature more!

NM: That is great advice. Jim, I am so appreciative of you. I am so grateful that you have chosen to invest your life the way that you are. You could have stayed in law and had a very meaningful life, but you chose to be intentionally purposeful in your path, and your path has led you where you are now. I so appreciate your heart for people and your willingness to make life better for others. I am thankful for you, Jim. I am thankful for the impact a leader can make when they choose to be intentional and purposeful.

AFTERWORD: NOW WHAT?

Now that you've read the 21 Priest Principles, learned about the character of Joseph, and listened in on my conversation with Dr. Mellor, the next step is up to you. How will you use this book in your own life? How will you develop the character needed to be a true servant leader? Permit me to offer some practical application suggestions.

Create a sheet with three columns and label them "Start", "Stop" and "Continue".

In the first column write three things you'd like to start doing after reading this book. A character trait you want to work on improving. A habit you want to develop.

In the second column list three things you want to stop, right now, based on what you've read. Maybe they are small things. A bad habit. A harmful attitude. Write down three things you need to put a halt to in order to develop into the leader you want to become.

Finally, you're probably doing some things right. List three of those good things and commit that you will keep doing them. Maintain the good values you have cultivated and build on them.

And if you're really committed to becoming a leader with character, find a trusted friend or mentor who will hold you accountable. Share these lists with them and ask them to check with you periodically to see how you're doing. Accountability is the key to seeing things through.

I pray God will use this book to deepen your character, enhance your leadership, positively impact others, and bring you success in the truest sense of the term.

ABOUT THE BOOK:

As an attorney, Jim Priest has witnessed what it takes to succeed in leadership and also how to fail in it. His observations and first hand experiences have led Priest to believe a leader's internal character is essential and responsible for both success and failure of the individual and organization they lead. Priest observed that many leaders neglect the importance of developing internal character, but do not fear, he has shared the twenty-one essentials and the explanation of the importance of character.

ABOUT THE AUTHOR:

Jim Priest is an attorney, minister, author, and executive coach. He currently serves as President of Sage Counsel PLLC and as President/Chief Executive Officer of Goodwill Industries of Central

Oklahoma. He has previously served as executive director of other non-profits. Priest likes to run, read, hike, write, and serves on several civic boards in his spare time. He has been married to his wondrous wife for forty-four years. The couple have two awesome adult children, a marvelous son in law and daughter in law, and a world changing grandson.